At ten o'clock P.M., all was quiet inside the home of Charles Lindbergh. The famous aviator lived with his wife, Anne, and their baby, Charles Jr., in rural New Jersey.

The Open Window

The baby's nurse, Betty Gow, followed her usual routine. Before going to bed, she tiptoed down the hall to check on Charles Jr.

Gow peeked into the baby's room. What she saw filled her with dread. The window was wide open and the crib was empty.

Charles Jr. was gone!

Gow ran to Lindbergh's study. "Do you have the baby?" she asked.

The Investigation

Frantic, the Lindberghs called the police. A search in and around their house turned up a few clues. They found a handwritten ransom note, muddy footprints, and a broken wooden ladder. But there was no sign of the baby.

Months passed, and the police were no closer to solving the case. They needed help. They called in a pair of handwriting experts to analyze the ransom note. The eyes of the world were watching.

The Question
How could handwriting experts help catch a kidnapper? Why are people often so obsessed with celebrities?

PREVIEW PHOTO
PAGE 1: **The Lindbergh home in Hopewell, New Jersey**

Book Design: Red Herring Design/NYC **Photo Credits:** Photographs © 2012: AP Images: 1, 15 right, 19 inset, 22, 23, 27, 34; Corbis Images: 32, 33, 36, 39, 41, 44 (Bettmann), 28 left (Library of Congress); Everett Collection, Inc.: 8; Getty Images: 42 right (Dorling Kindersley), 19 main (Gamma-Keystone-France), 42 center (Laurent Hamels), 13 (New York Times Co.), 10, 38 (NY Daily News Archive), 43 top right (Photodisc); Reprinted by permission of Glenbridge Publishing Ltd.: 29 right (from *Great Forgers and Famous Fakes*); Grant R. Sperry: 40; Media Bakery: back cover foreground (Steve Weisbauer), 3, 43 top left; Photo Researchers, NY/Phillipe Psaila: 43 bottom left; ShutterStock, Inc.: 30 (Janaka Dharmasena), cover, back cover background, 16 (jokerpro), 4, 5 (Denis and Yulia Pogostins), 14 background, 15 background (s_oleg), 42 bottom (tatniz); Smithsonian Institution Libraries/NASM/SI 71-109: 14 foreground, 15 left; The Image Works: 20 (Jesse Davidson Aviation Archive), 24 (Scherl/SV-Bilderdienst); Reprinted by permission of the University of Oklahoma Press, Norman: 28 right, 29 left (from *Forging History: The Detection of Fake Letters and Documents*, by Kenneth Rendell); VEER: 43 bottom right (Photodisc), 42 left (Stockbyte Photography).

Library of Congress Cataloging-in-Publication Data
Webber, Diane, 1968-
Celebrity son snatched : can cops catch the kidnapper? / Diane Webber.
p. cm. —
Includes bibliographical references and index.
ISBN-13 978-0-545-32810-4
ISBN-10 0-545-32810-1
1. Lindbergh, Charles Augustus, 1930-1932—Kidnapping, 1932—Juvenile literature. 2. Lindbergh, Charles A. (Charles Augustus), 1902-1974—Juvenile literature. 3. Hauptmann, Bruno Richard, 1899-1936—Juvenile literature. 4. Kidnapping—New Jersey—Hopewell—Juvenile literature.
5. Writing—Identification—Juvenile literature. 6. Graphology—Juvenile literature. I. Title.
HV6603.L5W39 2011
364.15'4092—dc22   2011006455

No part of this publication may be reproduced in whole or in part, or stored in a retrieval system, or transmitted in any form or by any means, electronic, mechanical, photocopying, recording, or otherwise, without written permission of the publisher. For information regarding permission, write to Scholastic Inc., 557 Broadway, New York, NY 10012.

Copyright © 2012, 2007 Scholastic Inc.
All Rights Reserved. Published by Scholastic Inc. Printed in the U.S.A.

SCHOLASTIC, XBOOKS, and associated logos are trademarks and/or registered trademarks of Scholastic Inc.

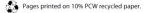 Pages printed on 10% PCW recycled paper.

1 2 3 4 5 6 7 8 9 10   40   21 20 19 18 17 16 15 14 13 12

CELEBRITY SON SNATCHED

Can Cops Catch the Kidnapper?

DIANE WEBBER

CHARLES LINDBERGH JR.

TABLE OF CONTENTS

PREVIEW **1**

CHAPTER 1
The Price of Fame 10
A historic flight puts a pilot in the spotlight.

Spirit of St. Louis **14**

CHAPTER 2
Kidnapped! 16
An open window. An empty crib. A missing baby.

CHAPTER 3
Evidence at Hand 24
Handwriting experts try to identify the kidnapper.

Real or Fake? **28**

CHAPTER 4
Follow the Money 30
Someone is spending the ransom money. Is it the kidnapper?

CHAPTER 5
Battle in the Court 34
Do the ransom notes match the suspect's handwriting?

XFILES **39**
- **Bad Handwriting** **40**
- **By the Letter** **42**
- **Brainwriting** **44**

1

The Price of Fame

A historic flight puts a pilot in the spotlight.

In 1927, just about everyone in America knew Charles Lindbergh's name.

On May 21 of that year, Lindbergh became the first person to fly nonstop across the Atlantic Ocean. He flew solo from New York to Paris, France. He made the 3,600-mile (5,800-kilometer) flight in his single-engine airplane, *Spirit of St. Louis*. The transatlantic trip took just over 33 hours.

Newspapers around the country announced his feat. Within days he was hailed as a hero. He became the most famous man in America. Wherever he went, fans surrounded him.

Fame and Fortune

Lindbergh's historic flight brought him more than fame. He also won a $25,000 prize. It was sponsored by Raymond Orteig, a wealthy Frenchman who owned hotels in New York City. In 1919, Orteig had offered the prize to the first aviator to fly nonstop from New York to Paris, or from Paris to New York.

Eight years later, Charles Lindbergh accepted Orteig's prize. He used his fame and his fortune to promote aviation.

But by the early 1930s, Lindbergh had grown tired of the attention. He and his wife, Anne Morrow Lindbergh, had just had their first child, a son named Charles Jr. The pilot decided that he wanted to be alone with his family. So he built a home near Hopewell, New Jersey. The large house was set in the woods at the end of a long driveway. At last, the family had privacy.

Then, on March 1, 1932, the family's peace and quiet was shattered.

ANNE MORROW LINDBERGH cradles her infant son, Charles Jr., in 1930.

Spirit of

Charles Lindbergh made his historic flight across the Atlantic Ocean in an airplane named *Spirit of St. Louis*. The plane was tiny and not very powerful. The cockpit was only three feet (94 cm) wide and 51 inches (130 cm) high. Lindbergh had to cut the top and bottom off of his flight map in order to eliminate extra weight.

Spirit of St. Louis is now on display at the National Air and Space Museum in Washington, D.C.

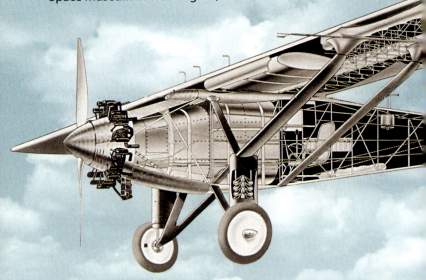

IN DEPTH

St. Louis

"The Spirit of St. Louis is a wonderful plane. It's like a living creature ..."

CHARLES LINDBERGH, 1927

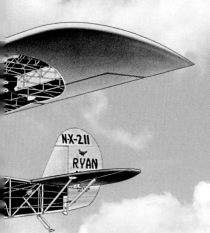

Stats:
Engines: 1 (223 horsepower)
Length: 27.7 ft. (8.4 meters)
Wingspan: 46 ft. (14 m)
Height: 9 ft., 10 inches (3 m)
Weight: 5,135 pounds
(2,329 kilograms)

2

Kidnapped!

**An open window.
An empty crib.
A missing baby.**

It began as a typical evening at the Lindbergh's home in rural New Jersey. At 10:00 P.M., the baby's nurse, Betty Gow, went to check on 20-month-old Charles Jr. But when Gow entered the baby's room, she was stunned. The baby wasn't in his crib! Gow ran to Lindbergh's study. "Do you have the baby?" she asked Lindbergh, alarmed. "Please don't fool me."

Lindbergh ran upstairs. He saw the empty crib. He saw an open window. "Anne!" he cried out to his wife. "They've stolen our baby."

"The Child Is in *Gute* Care"

The Lindberghs and Gow frantically searched the house for the baby. Charles Lindbergh found a handwritten note on the windowsill of his son's room. It read "Dear Sir! Have 50,000$ redy with 25000$ in 20$ bills 15000$ in 10$ bills and 10000$ in 5$ bills. After 2-4 days we will inform you were to deliver the Mony. We warn you for making anyding public or for notify the polise the child is in gute care."

Lindbergh called the police. When they arrived, Lindbergh gave them the note he had found. A police search in and around the house turned up more clues. They found muddy footprints on the floor of the baby's room. And they discovered a broken homemade ladder and footprints in the mud under the baby's window. But there was no sign of Charles Jr.

THIS RANSOM NOTE was left behind on the night that Charles Lindbergh Jr. (shown here) was kidnapped.

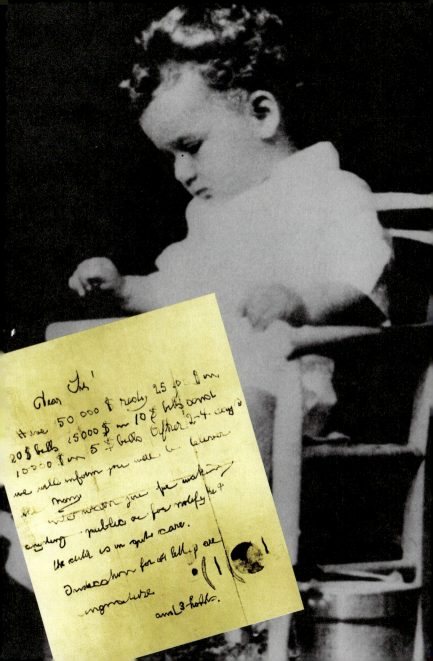

More Notes

On March 6, the Lindberghs received another ransom note. This one was postmarked March 4, Brooklyn, New York. The kidnapper was increasing the ransom from $50,000 to $70,000.

Two days later, Lindbergh's lawyer received a third ransom note. This one asked Lindbergh to communicate through notes in a newspaper.

Like the ransom note found on the night of the kidnapping, these notes contained misspelled words. For example, the note included the words *everyding*, *mony*, and *gute*, instead of "everything," "money," and "good."

POLICE DEPARTMENTS in more than 1,400 cities received this poster about the Lindbergh baby kidnapping.

An Offer to Help

John Condon was a retired New York City school principal. On March 8, he placed an item in a local newspaper, the *Bronx Home News*. In it, he offered to pay an additional $1,000 in ransom for the safe return of the Lindbergh baby. He also offered to act as a middleman between the kidnappers and the Lindberghs. The next day, the fourth ransom note was sent to Condon. The kidnappers accepted his offer to act as the middleman.

Around March 10, Lindbergh gave Condon $70,000. Lindbergh asked Condon to pay the ransom and get Charles Jr. back. Condon communicated with the kidnappers through newspaper articles. In the articles, he used the code name "Jafsie."

"John"

A few days and notes later, Condon agreed to meet a man who called himself John at a local cemetery. Condon asked for evidence that "John" knew where the Lindbergh's baby was. On March 16, Condon received the sleepwear Charles Jr. had been

NEW JERSEY OFFICIALS examine the clothing Charles Jr. had been wearing when he was kidnapped.

wearing the night he was kidnapped.

Condon continued to communicate with the kidnapper through ads in the paper. On the evening of April 2, Condon met with John again. They agreed to a reduced ransom of $50,000, which Condon handed to John.

Most of the money was in special bills called gold certificates. These would be easier to trace than regular bills. And the certificates' serial numbers had been recorded. This was done so investigators would be able to tell when and where the kidnapper spent the money.

In exchange, John gave Condon a receipt and a note with instructions for where to find the baby. The note said the baby was fine and could be found on a

A CROWD GATHERS near the area where the body of the Lindbergh baby was found in a shallow grave.

boat called the *Nelly*. It was near the island of Martha's Vineyard, Massachusetts.

Lindbergh was overjoyed. Soon he would have his son back. Lindbergh spent several weeks flying up and down the East Coast. But he couldn't find the *Nelly*.

Finally, on May 12, 1932, the search came to a tragic end. A truck driver was walking in the woods just a few miles from the Lindbergh home. He found the body of a baby. It was little Charles.

INDY'S BABY FOUND—SLAIN

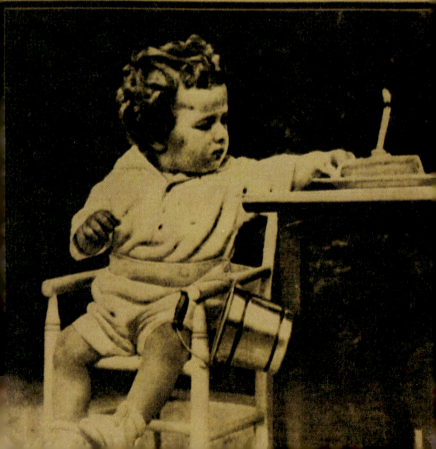

3

Evidence at Hand

Handwriting experts try to identify the kidnapper.

With the terrible discovery of the Lindbergh baby's body, the investigation changed. Now the police were looking for a murderer. And the whole country was watching.

The police sent the ransom notes to two handwriting experts, Wilmer T. Souder and Albert S. Osborn.

The police hoped to answer several questions. Were the notes written by a single kidnapper? Or were police looking for a gang of criminals? Could the experts tell anything about the writer from the notes?

Expert Review

Souder and Osborn studied the notes. They noticed:
- Words were misspelled in the same ways in all the notes. *Mony* (money), *singnature* (signature), and *ingnore* (ignore) were a few examples.
- Words like *light* and *right* were written with the g and h reversed ("lihgt" and "rihgt").
- The *t*'s, *i*'s, and *j*'s weren't crossed or dotted.

Both Souder and Osborn reached the same conclusion. One person had written all of the ransom notes.

Osborn thought the writer was German. The notes included the words *gute*, *aus*, and *dank*. These are the German words for "good," "out," and "thank."

Osborn created a paragraph with the key words in it. He told the police to read it to every suspect they found. The suspect would write down the words. Then the police would look for two things. Did the suspect's writing match the writing in the ransom notes? Did the suspect make the same spelling errors?

ndr. It is note necessary to punish
my code. Jim and M. Lindbergh know
ner Quyuam very well. we will keep
the child in ouer save plase until we
ave the money in hand, but if the deal
s note closed until the 8 of April we
will ask for 30 000 more. — aew note 70000
100000

        how can the Lindbergh follow
so many false clues he know, we
are heunst poly ouer singnature
is still the same as in the resumen
note but if Mr Lindbergh likes to
fool arround for another month
   we can help it.
      once he has to come to us anywa
but if he keeps on waiting we will doubll
    ouer amount that is absolute our form
abrudthechild
i is well

THE KIDNAPPER sent more than ten ransom notes to the Lindberghs or their middleman. All of them contained the same spelling and grammatical errors.

Real or Fake?

Document examiners know all the tricks for finding a forgery.

Joseph Cosey is one of history's greatest fakers. He forged documents by Benjamin Franklin, Abraham Lincoln, and other famous people. Cosey died around 1950. But his forgeries are still floating around today.

How can an expert tell a Cosey fake from the real thing?

It's a two-step process. First, document examiners look at the materials used to create the questioned document. They check to make sure the paper, ink, and stamps are from the right time period.

Next they look at the writing itself. How? They check it against a document that everyone knows is real.

Examiners compare the two documents to see whether the writing matches. The list on the facing page shows some of the things they look for. Below, you can see how to tell a forgery from the real thing.

ABRAHAM LINCOLN (left) and his original letter (right)

Lincoln's letter was written quickly. Words flow to the right.

The letters aren't well formed.

There's a lot of space between the lines.

Look at the signature. Lincoln's "A" goes below the baseline. And the last "n" was a little higher than the rest of his letters.

IN DEPTH

1. Is the writing **SMOOTH?** Shaky writing can mean that someone is writing slowly—and copying someone else's handwriting.
2. **HEIGHT?** Forgers often make their letters smaller than those of the person they're copying.
3. **LIFT?** Do both the author and the forger lift their pens between words?
4. **CONNECT?** Do they both connect capital and lowercase letters?
5. **FORM?** Are any letters written in a strange way?
6. **PRESSURE?** Do the author and the forger put the same amount of pressure on their pens?
7. **SLANT?** Does their writing lean in the same direction?
8. **BASELINE?** Do they both write in a straight line?
9. **DOTS AND CROSSES?** Do they dot their *i*'s and cross their *t*'s the same way?
10. **EXTRA EFFORT?** Are the letters corrected or traced over? This may be a sign of a forgery.

JOSEPH COSEY (right) and his forgery (below)

Cosey's letter was written slowly. Words are more up-and-down. They don't flow together.

The letters are carefully written.

There isn't a lot of space between the lines.

All the letters of the signature are on the same line.

4

Follow the Money

Someone is spending the ransom money. Is it the kidnapper?

For two years, the investigation into the Lindbergh kidnapping stalled. As far as anyone could tell, no one had spent the ransom money.

Then, in September 1934, the police finally got an important lead. A gas station manager had received a gold certificate worth $10 from a customer. He stared at it. The government had stopped using these bills a year before. Was it fake?

"What's wrong?" asked the customer. The manager noticed that he had a German accent. The manager said that nothing was wrong. But as the car pulled away, he wrote the license plate number down on the bill. Then he took the money to the bank.

A clerk at the bank was also curious. He checked a pamphlet that the Bureau of Investigation had printed. (This agency is now called the Federal Bureau of Investigation, or FBI. It investigates crimes against the United States.) The pamphlet contained all the serial numbers on the Lindbergh ransom bills.

The bill's serial number was in the pamphlet. The bill was part of the ransom money!

Tracking Down a Suspect

Government officials traced the license plate number to the owner of the car. His name was Bruno Richard

Hauptmann. He was a German-born carpenter. The police arrested him. Was he the "John" who had taken the ransom bills that night in the graveyard? Witnesses said he was.

The police searched Hauptmann's home. They found $14,000 of the ransom cash hidden in his garage. They also noticed that a beam—a long, heavy piece of wood—was missing from the attic. The wood from the remaining beams matched the wood of the homemade ladder that had been found outside the Lindbergh's house.

Hauptmann insisted he was innocent. He said that a friend named Isidor Fisch had given him the money for safekeeping. Fisch had gone back to Germany a about a year before. Hauptmann said he knew nothing about the kidnapping.

The police wanted to see Hauptmann's handwriting.

THE HOMEMADE LADDER used in the kidnapping was made of wood that matched wooden beams in the floor of Hauptmann's attic.

LAWYERS COMPARE WORDS from the ransom notes with words written by Bruno Hauptmann.

5

Battle in the Court

Do the ransom notes match the suspect's handwriting?

The police questioned Bruno Hauptmann for a long time. Then they made him write for hours. He wrote down a sample passage that Albert Osborn had created. He also rewrote some of the ransom notes. The police made him do each test three times, with three different pens.

Investigators also gathered samples of Hauptmann's

handwriting from his home. The experts compared this evidence to the ransom notes. Hauptmann wrote the words *to* and *the* in unusual ways. So did the notewriter. Hauptmann's *y*'s looked like *v*'s with a stick added at the bottom. So did the *y*'s on the ransom notes.

Most of the experts reached the same conclusion: Hauptmann had written the ransom notes.

In court, Osborn and Souder testified against Hauptmann.

The defense attorney representing Hauptmann produced one handwriting expert. His name was John Trendley. Trendley said he doubted that Hauptmann had written the first ransom note. Would the jury agree?

Nailed by the Notes

The trial of Bruno Richard Hauptmann began on January 2, 1935,

WAS ISIDOR FISCH (left) involved in the kidnapping? No one will ever know.

in Flemington, New Jersey. Throngs of reporters and spectators filled the town. The jurors took just 11 hours to reach a decision. They found Hauptmann guilty of first-degree murder. On April 3, 1936, he was executed for the murder of Charles Lindbergh Jr.

Case Closed

The case was solved. Or was it? Many questions remain unanswered. Where was the rest of the ransom money? And had Hauptmann's friend Isidor Fisch been involved in the crime? Fisch died in Germany in 1934. No one ever had a chance to question him.

Also, what role had public opinion played in the case? The police had been under tremendous pressure to solve a case involving an American hero. What's more, the United States had fought against Germany in World War I, which had ended in 1918. There was still plenty of anti-German feeling around. Had the police perhaps framed Hauptmann, a German immigrant?

According to at least one later investigation, Hauptmann did have a hand in the crime. A TV show called *Forensic Files* sent the handwriting evidence from the case to three experts. They all came to the same conclusions: The same person had written the ransom notes. And that person was most likely Bruno Richard Hauptmann. ✘

HANDWRITING ANALYSIS helped convict Bruno Hauptmann (above) of the kidnapping and murder of Charles Lindbergh Jr.

BAD HANDWRITING	40
BY THE LETTER	42
BRAINWRITING	44
RESOURCES	46
GLOSSARY	47
INDEX	48

X FILES

Bad Handwriting

Forensic document examiner Grant Sperry is on the hunt for frauds.

GRANT SPERRY runs Forensic Document Examination Services in Germantown, Tennessee.

How did you get started?
SPERRY: I was a special agent with the Army Criminal Investigations Command. I developed an interest in all types of frauds.

What other training have you had?
SPERRY: I did a two-year training with the Army Lab. I've done courses with the CIA (Central Intelligence Agency), the Secret Service, and the FBI. You have to constantly keep educating yourself.

What do you like about your job?
SPERRY: I learn something new on every single case. And I get great satisfaction out of solving issues in a way that helps somebody. Every morning I wake up and think, "I get to go to the lab."

IN DEPTH

You analyzed the ransom notes from the Lindbergh case. What was that like?

SPERRY: I was surprised by how much evidence there was! I used software called Write On. That really helped my analysis. Once I scanned in all the documents, I could do searches. I could ask for all the *th* combinations, for example. Then I could compare them all.

What did you learn about the kidnapper Bruno Hauptmann?

SPERRY: He disguised his handwriting the same way— every time. That's very unusual. He probably did something very simple, like holding the pen differently. That way it's easy to write the same way every time.

What do you have to say to students who might be interested in forensic document examination?

SPERRY: Great! We need more good forensic scientists. Go to the American Academy of Forensic Sciences website. It's www.aafs.org. We have a Young Forensic Scientists Forum. It will tell you how to get involved in the subject.

By the Letter

Check out a forensic document examiner's tools of the trade.

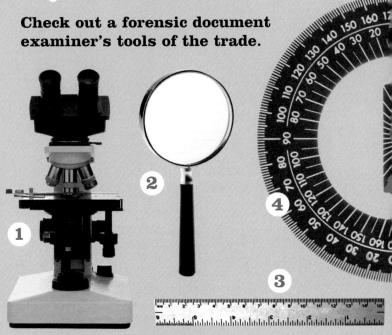

1 Binocular microscope Experts use this microscope to examine the ink on a suspicious document. It also helps reveal whether the letters have been traced over.

2 Magnifying glass A document examiner's key tool. It's used to look closely at individual letters.

3 Ruler It's used to measure whether the letters are written on an even baseline.

4 Protractor Experts use a protractor to measure the slant of a writer's letters.

5 Cameras Experts photograph suspicious and genuine documents. They then use the images to compare the two.

IN DEPTH

6 Document examination systems
Experts use these machines to look at documents with infrared (IR) and ultraviolet (UV) light. IR and UV light can reveal hidden marks on a document.

7 Light box
Suspicious documents are often examined on a light box. The light picks up evidence of tracing. It also reveals a lot about the ink the writer used.

8 Office equipment
Good document examiners know their equipment. They can often trace a document to the machine that produced it.

Brainwriting

Does your handwriting show what's going on in your head?

Graphologists study handwriting. They say it reveals information about the writer. Graphology isn't a real science. No evidence has been found that shows a link between handwriting and personality. But it can be fun. Look at your handwriting and answer the questions below. Then analyze graphology for yourself.

1. Where do you cross your *t*'s?

¾ of the way up: You're realistic about your goals.
Very high: You're reaching for the stars.
Very low: You could be feeling down.

2. How do you dot your *i*'s?

Close to the stem: You're very detailed.
High over the stem: You're patient with details.
Missing completely: You have trouble remembering things you're supposed to finish.
With a circle: You want to stand out, but you're also looking for acceptance.

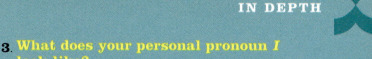

IN DEPTH

3. **What does your personal pronoun *I* look like?**

   Well balanced, with both an upper loop and a lower hook: You probably have a good relationship with your parents.

   A "stick figure," written with a single stroke: You're an independent person.

   Printed, not in cursive: Another sign of independence.

   Very large: You're confident and take up a lot of personal space.

   Very small: You don't like to draw a lot of attention to yourself.

4. **How crowded is your writing?**
   Very crowded: You may be shy and withdrawn.
   Takes up the whole page: You have a lot of confidence.

5. **How big are your letters?**
   Small and neat: You are very focused and controlled.
   Huge: Chances are you're loose and carefree.

6. **Do you write the way you were taught in school?**
   Yes, the letters look perfect: You're good at following rules.
   No, the letters are unusual: You're very creative.
   No, the writing is sloppy: You may not be well organized.

RESOURCES

Here's a selection of books and websites for more information about the Lindbergh case, handwriting analysis, and forensic science.

What to Read Next

NONFICTION

Edwards, Judith. *The Lindbergh Baby Kidnapping in American History.* Berkeley Heights, NJ: Enslow Publishers, 2000.

Ellen, David. *Scientific Examination of Documents.* Boca Raton, FL: CRC Press, 2005.

Lane, Brian, and Laura Buller. *Crime and Detection* (DK Eyewitness Books). New York: DK Publishing, 2005.

Lowe, Sheila. *The Complete Idiot's Guide to Handwriting Analysis.* New York: Alpha Books, 2007.

Martin, Michael. *Handwriting Evidence.* Mankato, MN: Capstone Press, 2007.

Platt, Richard. *Crime Scene: The Ultimate Guide to Forensic Science.* New York: DK Publishing, 2003.

Shulz, Karen K. *CSI Expert! Forensic Science for Kids.* Waco, TX: Prufrock Press Inc., 2008.

Webber, Diane. *Do You Read Me? Famous Cases Solved by Handwriting Analysis!* New York: Franklin Watts, 2007.

FICTION

Bryant, Jen. *The Trial.* New York: Yearling, 2005.

Hein, E. K. *The Forensic Mission: Investigate Forensic Science Through a Killer Mystery!* Hoboken, NJ: Wiley Publishing Inc., 2007.

Websites

CSI: The Experience: Web Adventures
http://forensics.rice.edu

This site is part of an exhibit that has traveled to science museums around the country. It immerses you in hands-on science while leading you through the challenge of solving a crime mystery.

Handwriting Analysts Group
www.handwriting.org

This website is a great introduction to graphology.

Lindbergh: The American Experience
www.pbs.org/wgbh/amex/lindbergh

This is the companion site to the Charles Lindbergh episode of the PBS series *The American Experience.*

GLOSSARY

analyze (AN-uh-lize) *verb* to examine something carefully in order to understand it

aviator (AY-vee-ay-tur) *noun* a person who flies aircraft

baseline (BAYSS-line) *noun* the bottom of a line of writing

document (DOK-yoo-mehnt) *noun* a paper or collection of papers with any kind of writing on it

evidence (EV-uh-duhnss) *noun* information and facts that help prove something

execute (EK-suh-kyoot) *verb* to kill someone as punishment for a crime

first-degree murder (FURST-duh-gree MUR-dur) *noun* murder that is planned and deliberate

forensic (fuh-REHN-zik) *adjective* describing the science used to investigate and solve crimes

forgery (FORJ-uhr-ree) *noun* a fake or copied document, signature, or work of art

fraud (FRAWD) *noun* the act of cheating or tricking someone

graphology (Graf-OL-uh-gee) *noun* the study of handwriting to understand personality

handwriting analysis (HAND-rye-ting uh-NAL-uh-siss) *noun* the careful, step-by-step study of writing done by hand

jury (JU-ree) *noun* a group of people who listen to a court case and decide whether someone is guilty or innocent

middleman (MID-UHL MAN) *noun* a person who arranges business or deals between other people

perp (PURP) *noun* slang for *perpetrator*, a person who commits a crime

ransom (RAN-suhm) *noun* money demanded in exchange for releasing someone held captive

rural (RUR-uhl) *adjective* in or relating to the countryside

serial number (SEER-ee-ul NUM-bur) *noun* a series of numbers that identifies an item

testify (TESS-tuh-fye) *verb* to state the truth or give evidence in court

INDEX

American Academy of Forensic Science, 41
arrest, 32–33

binocular microscopes, 42, *42*
Bronx Home News newspaper, 21
Bureau of Investigation, 32

cameras, 42, *43*
Condon, John, 21, 22
Cosey, Joseph, 28, *29*

document examination systems, 43, *43*
document examiners, 25, 26, 28–29, 36, 38, 40–41, *40*, 41–42, 43, *43*

evidence, 18, 21–22, *27*, 35–36, 38, 40–41
execution, 37

Federal Bureau of Investigation (FBI), 32, 40
Fisch, Isidor, 33, *36*, 37
Forensic Files (television show), 38
forgeries, 28–29, *28–29*

gold certificates, 22, 31, 32
Gow, Betty, 17, 18
graphologists, 44–45

handwriting, *28–29*, 29, 33, *34*, 35–36, 38, 41, 44–45, *44*, *45*
handwriting experts. *See* document examiners.
Hauptmann, Bruno Richard, 33, *34*, 35–36, 36–37, 38, *38*, 41

infrared (IR) light, 43

"John," 21–22, 33
jury, 36–37

ladder, 18, *32–33*, 33
light boxes, 43, *43*
Lindbergh, Anne Morrow, 12, *13*, 18
Lindbergh, Charles, *10*, 11–12, 12–13, 14, *15*, 15, 17–18, 20, 21, 23, 38
Lindbergh, Charles Jr., 12, *13*, 17–18, *19*, *20*, 21–22, *22*, 22–23, *23*, *24*, 25, 37
Lindbergh home, 12–13, 17, 23

magnifying glasses, 42, *42*
National Air and Space Museum, 14
Nelly (boat), 23
newspapers, 12, 20, 21, 22, *24*

office equipment, 43, *43*
Orteig, Raymond, 12
Osborn, Albert S., 25, 26, 35, 36

personalities, 44–45
police, 18, *20*, 25–26, 31, 33, 35–36, 37–38
protractors, 42, *42*
public opinion, 37–38

ransom money, 18, 20, 21, 22, 31–32, 33
ransom notes, 18, *19*, 20, 21, 25–26, *27*, *34*, 35, 36, 38, 40–41
rulers, 42, *42*

serial numbers, 22, 32
sleepwear, 21–22, *22*
Souder, Wilmer T., 25, 26, 36
Sperry, Grant, 40–41, *40*
Spirit of St. Louis (airplane), 11, 14–15, *14–15*
suspects, 26, 33, 35–36

tools, 40, 42–43, *42*, *43*
tracing, 29, 42, 43
transatlantic flight, 11–12, 14
Trendley, John, 36
trial, 36–37

ultraviolet (UV) light, 43

wanted poster, *20*
witnesses, 33
World War I, 38
Write On software, 40

48